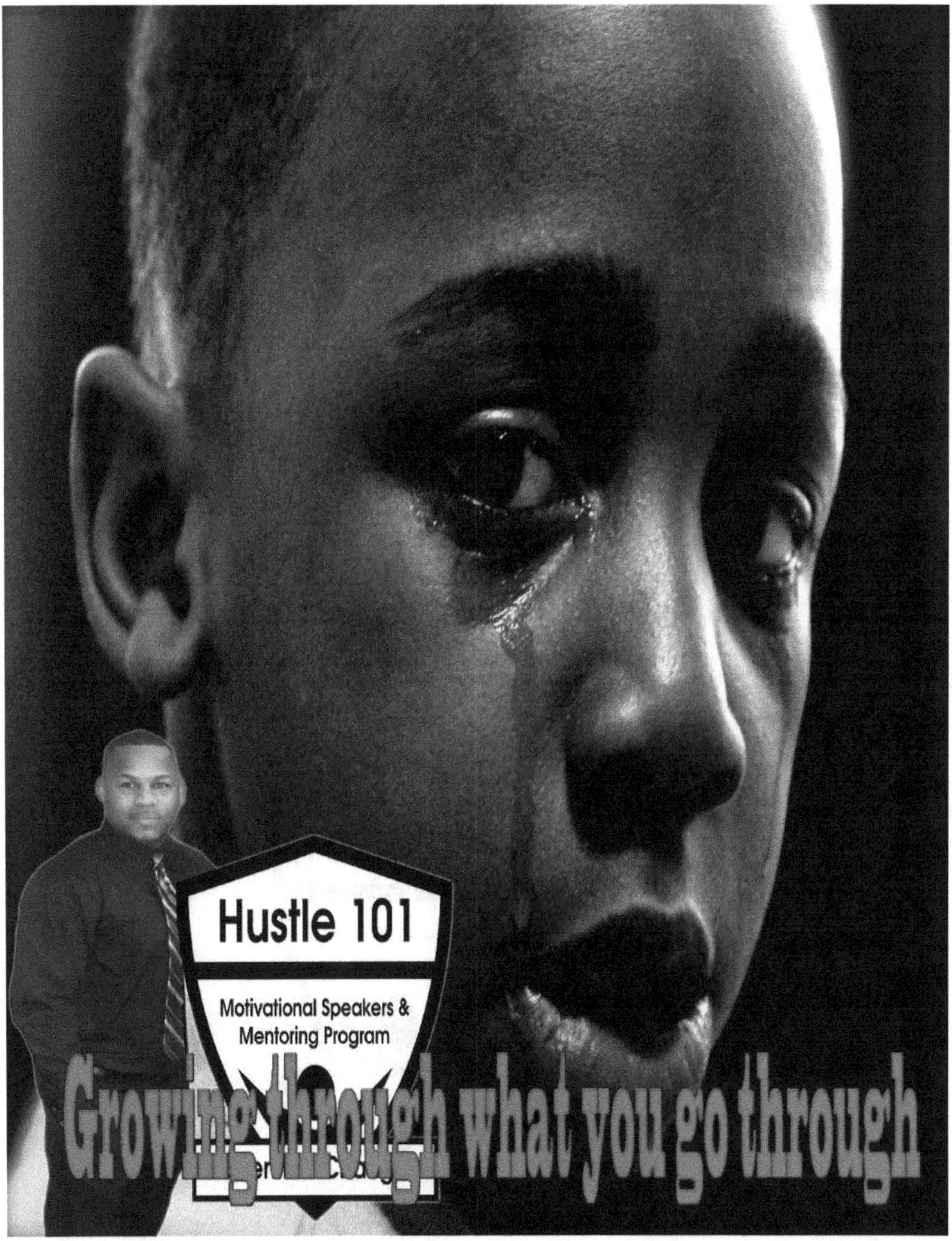
Hustle 101
Motivational Speakers &
Mentoring Program
Growing through what you go through

Growing through what you go through

Copyright © 2021 by Santiego Rivers

All rights reserved. This book may not be reproduced or transmitted in any form without the written permission of the author.

"no copyright infringement is intended."

ISBN 978-1-7376037-5-7

We are all one struggle away from our breaking point. One setback away from not being able to continue the path that we were destined to take.

Sometimes the hardest thing to face is the one thing we need to address to reclaim our peace of mind.

Hard lessons help us understand that certain things in our lives must fall apart so everything else can come together the way it is supposed to.

We may not like to face this truth, but running from our fears will eventually bring us face-to-face with our most profound agony. We can't run from ourselves.

The pain, struggles, heartaches, and losses that we face in our life are part of the bigger plan to make us stronger to overcome the obstacles that we will face in life.

Life doesn't get easier; we learn to get stronger. We get better!

This book will reveal the one thing that we forget when we are facing our most challenging battles.

We are not alone in our times of grief and sorrow.

God doesn't get us through the storm; he gives us the strength to endure until it's time for us to move past the obstacles in our life. God's love and wisdom are the gifts that will guide us through our tough times.

Pain will always give us gifts. That gift will go unnoticed during adversity, but it will be evident when we come through that storm.

Life doesn't get easier; we learn to get stronger. We get better!

Truthfully speaking, if we are speaking truthfully, losing someone you love is the hardest thing to overcome alone.

I've lost people in my life that I felt that I desperately needed when I was trying to figure out what my life will eventually become.

How do you say goodbye when you haven't even found the words to tell the person you love how much they mean to your life?

How do you let go when your mind, heart, and soul still hold onto the memories that made you smile in your darkest of hours?

How do you begin to cope or understand something that you don't fully understand yourself?

It's one thing facing or coping with loss when you are an adult, but how does a child deal or overcome with losing a loved one?

Losing a loved one makes you feel helpless, which brings forth many other feelings and emotions that refuse to stay buried inside.

I buried feelings and emotions that would eventually find its' way out regardless of how much I tried to hold them in.

Grief in children is seen in many forms. I know this for a fact because I went through all of them while trying to cope and understand why I lost someone in my life that made me feel special.

Common grief reactions in children can include the following:

- Changes in eating, sleeping, and relationships
- Emotional outburst
- Increase in negative behaviors
- Changes in school performance, both negative and positive
- Regression in developmental abilities
- Physical complaints including, headache, stomachache, muscle aches, and more
- Inability to identify and express feelings about the death

Let me tell you about the obstacles that I had to overcome.

Losing my grandfather changed my life. He was the superman who made me dream that I could come close to be half the man he was in my life one day.

I remember watching my grandfather work in the garage on cars and how amazing it was to see him perform.

I used to put on his cologne and wear his shoes even though I knew that I couldn't wear them.

I tried to eat what my grandfather ate and drink what he drank even though I needed a lot of sugar with my small cup of coffee.

I loved when the weekend would come because I knew that I would be heading to my grandparents' house and spend time with my grandfather.

He was the alpha and the omega that centered my universe. His departure from my life was like a black hole swallowing what was and what will ever be in my life.

Many things in my life changed when I lost my grandfather, but one thing remained the same. I was hurting inside, and I didn't have anyone to turn to. The loss of my grandfather tore my world into pieces.

I stopped eating, but my sleeping increased. When my eyes were open, I made sure that I did whatever it took to close them as soon as possible.

It's funny how a child learns how particular medications can make you tired and allow you to close your eyes even if you can't sleep in peace.

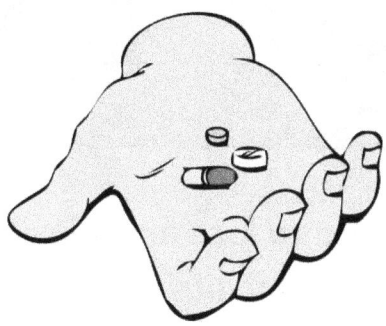

I was willing to deal with restless nights than face the reality of not having my grandfather in my life when my eyes were open. So, I slept as much as possible, but the pain remained.

I became an introvert pushing away friends and family because I didn't want to get close to anyone who could be taken away from me before I was ready to let them go.

I couldn't afford to lose anyone else out of my life.

I became angry and upset, and I didn't know why. I was angry and upset with myself for being angry and upset, and it just made me even more angry and upset.

Just in case you didn't fully understand what I said, let me repeat it for clarity.

I was angry and upset with myself for being angry and upset, and it just made me even more angry and upset.

Eventually, I became angry and upset with the people around me because I was tired of being angry and upset with myself.

I wanted someone else to feel the pain and the hurt that I was feeling inside because the feeling was killing me.

My emotional outburst was aimed at anyone and everyone who was in my vicinity.

I learned that hurt people hurt people, and I was hurting inside.

I tried hurting myself, which eventually moved into hurt those around me. This is probably why I closed myself off to being around other people.

They say miserable people love company; I will be the first person to disagree. I just wanted to be alone.

The only person that I needed in my life was no longer there. So, what do you do when you realize that you are alone?

You find ways to cope with the pain that often makes you act out of character.

I got into fights in my neighborhood which would eventually make its way into school. I was kicked out of my regular school and sent to an alternative school for my increased negative behavior.

I was fighting because I was lashing out. After all, I was hurting on the inside.

Before the Assistant principal sent me to the alternative school, my grades dropped, and my school performance was greatly affected.

I have always liked school, and I knew that I could do the work, but I had never healed from losing my grandfather, and I didn't have anyone to tell about the pain I was feeling inside.

Being sent to that alternative school helped me stop lashing out at other people and start my long hard look into the depth of my soul.

As I started to look inwards, I noticed that the pain I was dealing with put a regression in my development abilities.

Before losing my grandfather, I was brave and fearless. But I became scared and doubtful of myself and my abilities.

My mind was failing me, which led to my body being in so much pain. As a result, I had migraine headaches that followed me into my adult years.

I suffered from stomachaches, muscle aches, and pain. So how does a once healthy child become someone who is always sick?

Your mind and body attacking you are what happens when you try to bury something inside that you were never meant to hold onto or keep inside.

After eventually finding someone to open to, I understood that my symptoms and anger were coming from my Inability to identify and express my feelings about death.

How does a child process death when they don't even know the beauty and the meaning of life?

Losing my grandfather made me think long and hard about life. When you are left to figure things out on your own, sometimes you make many wrong decisions that you pray you will have the opportunity to live and grow through.

Talking with someone gave me a whole new perspective about death and losing someone close to me.

They taught me about caterpillars and the stages that they must go through to become a butterfly. I would later write a book about becoming a butterfly and the steps along the way, which reminds us to trust the process as we take our journey in life.

Butterflies are a symbol of the transformation we go through during our grief journey.

Grief is a journey that we should never face alone. Whether the loss was expected or sudden, the pain still hurt those left to process the loss.

The loss of a loved one requires grieving and mourning. Grief is what you think and feel on the inside after someone you love and care about dies.

I didn't know what to think, but I do know that I felt empty inside. This feeling would last me a long time until I moved to the mourning stage.

Mourning is the outward expression of those thoughts and feelings. My outward mourning was highlighted with my anger and aggression towards others because I got tired of causing myself so much pain.

Blue symbolizes our sadness, and **butterflies** symbolize hope and healing.

Looking at **_blue butterflies_** helps remind me that the loss of a loved one will always be a part of my life, but it does not have to be something that continues to bring me pain.

After the **grief** and the **mourning** comes the **healing** if you learn to trust the process along the way.

Hope and healing come from talking to someone about our sadness and pain, which will not disappear without help.

Healing is a process that will not happen overnight, but it will happen if you open and let your pain and emotions out.

Find someone to talk to because it always helps to let it out. When you let out all the pain, and the sadness will start the process of your healing. It did for me.

We must learn to be thankful for the rain if we hope to eventually experience the joy of seeing a rainbow in our lives.

I have experienced my share of storms that have produced some of the most beautiful rainbows I have ever seen.

It took me learning to trust even when I didn't fully understand everything that I was feeling inside and the process I was going through chasing my rainbow.

I had to accept that many things were more significant and complex than my understanding which I often connected to my feelings and emotions.

The pain and losses that I had endured in my life made me do and act in ways that I knew wouldn't bring honor and respect to my grandfathers' memory.

I would have been ashamed for my grandfather to see me do the things I did while dealing with losing him.

I learned that who we are and the things that we do reflects on the people that we love because even when they are not able to be present, they are still in our life as we carry them in our heart, mind, and soul.

Our actions reflect the things that they taught us when they were physically present in our life.

How we treat other people and how we carry ourselves reflects the values instilled in us by the people we love.

After being reminded of these things gave me comfort. I found comfort in knowing that my grandfather is still with me in my memories and the skills that he taught me when he was present in my life.

Jutta Bauer
Winner of the Hans Christian Andersen Award for illustration

I feel that he is now my guardian angel, that voice of reason that makes me think before acting out of character.

My grandfather is the thought that makes me pause and think before I act out of anger instead of responding with love when my emotions are not balanced.

When things in my life don't make sense, I smile and think about one of the most incredible men that I ever knew and how he would respond and feel, knowing that I am always trying to be the best version of myself.

These are the things that I feel will make my grandfather happy and give me peace of mind in my darkest of hours.

This book is dedicated to anyone who has lost someone important in their life. No one knows the exact pain you feel inside, but people can help you reach peace with your emotions.

Please seek counseling and find someone to talk to, vent to that is willing to listen to you as you find a positive way to release all the negative energy you are holding onto.

The Blue Butterfly Family Grief Center is a Tidewell Hospice program that supports grieving children and teens, ages 5-18, after the death of a significant person in their lives.

Mental health professionals and trained volunteers facilitate the Blue Butterfly groups. The facilitators use evidence-based interventions that support children and families on their grief journey.

Even if you do not get help from The Blue Butterfly Family Grief Center, please seek counseling somewhere and find someone to talk to.

Getting help is something that your lost love one would want for you.

https://tidewellhospice.org/home/programs/grief-support/blue-butterfly/

www.ingramcontent.com/pod-product-compliance
Lightning Source LLC
Chambersburg PA
CBHW071014160426
43193CB00012B/2047